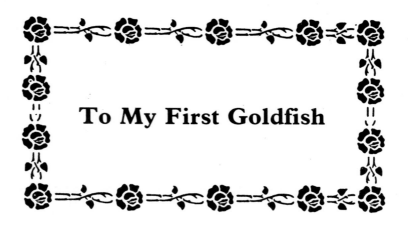

To My First Goldfish

Front endpapers
The garden pool opens up a new world of fish combined with plants and flowers and every garden is enhanced by the cool aquatic scenery.

Back endpapers
Goldfish are graceful and colorful and bring life to your garden pool. Photo by A. Roth.

Title page: The golds and reds and rainbow colors of domesticated pool fishes are the result of years of selective breeding of hardy goldfish and koi.

A Beginner's Guide to
Garden Pools

Written by
Dr. Herbert R. Axelrod

Contents

1.
Why Garden Pools?

There are three principal reasons why people have pools of fishes in their gardens:
1. They enjoy fishes and want to have live pets which require less care than dogs, cats, or birds. They want

Japanese pool gardens are a way of life to their owners. Photo courtesy of Kodansha Ltd.

color that almost no other living thing has in such variety and which is within their ability to purchase.

2. They have a lowland garden which accumulates water and encourages mosquito production, offensive smells and dampness in their cellars and the best way to cure this problem is to dig a deep pool and create a garden pool with beautiful flowers in and around it. Flowers which, by the way, make the garden pool worthwhile in itself since there are dozens, perhaps even hundreds, of colorful and interesting water lilies, lotus, iris and many other plants associated with garden pools suitable to both temperate and tropical zones of the world.

3. For profit...many people are profit (money) oriented and if they can have a hobby which brings in a little money, that makes it more interesting. Garden pools can be used to raise all kinds of fishes, especially tropical aquarium fishes like mollies, platies, guppies and swordtails, in the summer...goldfish and koi in the winter. These pools also can produce water lilies which can be sold as cut flowers, or the tubers can be harvested each fall and sold as roots to other water gardeners. One enterprising fellow has a chain of seven water gardens which produce plants and *daphnia*. *Daphnia* are small water bugs which are fed to aquarium fish. His local petshop buys all he can produce...and *Daphnia* never leave the water the way mosquito larvae do when they "hatch" into flying insects.

So, when you have decided on which aspect of the garden pool hobby interests you, then and only then can you design your pool, for there are different designs for each of the three objectives and building your garden pool by yourself can be easy and fun but only if it is carefully pre-planned.

Many builders and developers offer garden pools in many residential developments. The value of a formal garden pool, of permanent construction, is usually reflected in the selling price of a home. Keep this in mind when constructing your own garden pool. Perhaps by adding a little more time and money, you might have an expense which is recaptured in the value of your home.

The Garden Pool Without the Garden

Many restaurants, searching for unusual decors, have constructed a moat or shallow water raceway around their premises. Into this body of water they introduce large koi and goldfish. Powerful filters, the kind used for swimming pools, keep the water very clear, thus making the fishes visible. The usual pool of this sort is less than 18 inches deep. Plants, if they have any, are usually restricted to large pots protruding out of the moat, or the moat is S-shaped and the plants are located in the land portion of the S-shape.

The value of these moat ponds has recently been extolled by one owner in Fort Lauderdale, Florida. He claims the moats have cut down on trespassers, thus cutting down on thefts; he also feels safer in case of fire, since the pond around his restaurant inhibits the fire spreading to the rest of his buildings. On top of these extra values, he feels that when patrons have to wait for a table, they don't mind waiting outdoors where they and their children can watch the fish. The moats are usually lit at night and this soft lighting reflects onto the building itself and adds glamor that floodlighting fails to achieve.

Moat ponds must be made of cement, usually poured and formed to the shape desired. Bridges over the pond ensure that all parts of the moat are visible from above, though the bridges merely go over the contour of the moat but not across it. Think of a dollar sign, $. . . the bridges would be the lines with the moat being the $ thus all the crossings except one would be in a north-south direction. The exception would be the bridge going into the building which the moat surrounds.

Filters, and filters with built-in heaters, are available from any swimming pool supplier. As a matter of fact, the people who install custom built swimming pools might be the ones to employ for the entire project.

The moat should be as covered as possible. This will keep the water from overheating in the sun, and provide some shade for the fish. If a building is designed with a moat, the roof of the building usually can overhang the moat. The sun will merely assist the growth of algae on the cement, coloring it a very pleasing dark green. The filter should be changed frequently and the filter medium should probably be diatomaceous earth. Petshops carry such filters but they are usually too small for moats.

Most large koi ponds are built this way since deep ponds hide the fishes and, after all, viewing the fishes seems to be the major reason for the garden pool in the first place.

Where To Put Your Pool

Before you can make an intelligent decision about the location of your garden pool, you should consider alternatives. It is clear that once the pool is set up moving it might be extremely difficult, if not impossible.

Koi and goldfish require feeding with prepared flake and pellet foods which are available at your local pet store.

To be thorough about it, list all the likely locations that have the following characteristics:

1. The ground is level.
2. The ground is soft and easily dug into and without large rocks.
3. The location receives direct sunlight at least half a day, but not necessarily the whole day. (Unless the pool is more than 30 inches deep, it might overheat if it receives direct sunlight all day).
4. It is not close to a building foundation which might suffer should the pond leak.
5. It can be protected from dogs and children, among others, falling in.
6. It has enough room around it so you can walk all around it; you'll want to see the fish from all angles, and you'll want to reach the plants as easily as possible.

After you have listed the various areas possible for locating your garden pool, discuss it with your family and friends. Evaluate the location in terms of the six criteria mentioned above. Only then can you continue with the development stage of garden pond construction.

2.
Variations

In the previous section you decided where to locate your pond. In this process you also had some idea of how large a pond you really want. Ponds are measured in their cubic contents, just like an aquarium...and just

Almost any garden can accommodate a pool; the size, shape and style are dictated by the available land.

like an aquarium, the larger the pond, the easier it is to care for.

How large? The perfect pond for your garden is somewhere between too large and too small. The "too large" refers to your budget, while the "too small" refers to the available land. Making rules as to size is difficult, but one that the author has used for many years is that the pool should be large enough to hold the largest member of the family with his or her arms outstretched; it should not be deeper than the shortest member of the family. Its cost should be about 2% of the current value of the home which it is to grace.

Now, with these parameters, you will be able to proceed with your plans. An architect, or even someone with a little building or masonry experience, can help you decide whether you want a **formal** pool or an **informal** pond.

A formal pool is usually the center of attraction of a formal garden. Many contain statues and fountains; many are circular, oval or rectangular. The author has one which has no side equal to any of the others...and is a hexagon (six sides). It has about 75 square feet of surface and a depth of 42 inches. It is surrounded with a sitting wall about 18″ high, that's two cement blocks high. People like to sit and watch the fishes, especially in the summer when the fry scoot around. The sitting wall also keeps out kids, though one of my neighbors had an inquisitive dog who jumped over the low wall and eventually landed inside the goldfish pool. Luckily for him we were sleeping with the door open and heard him screaming. I dragged him out at 3 o'clock in the morning, his belly full of water. He never visited our yard again. From time to time we find other small animals which drowned in the pool, usually rodents. So, pools without fences can be dangerous but that's one of the problems with small formal pools. There is just not enough room to build steps to aid an animal to escape from the pond.

The **informal** pond, however, is just that. It's a pond and not a pool. As with almost all ponds, it looks natural, is usually found at the lowest level in the terrain, has slowly receding banks, thus dogs and other animals are hardly likely to drown, and usually costs less to make than a formal pool.

The formal pool

Formal pools have many advantages over the fake ponds we refer to as informal pools. First, they usually require a lot more skill to make than an informal pond and thus require (usually) professional help. Formal ponds are usually geometric in design. Their shape is usually a circle, oval or rectangle. They can be made to almost any reasonable depth and they can be made to match the architecture of the home which they are to grace.

Formal pools are usually much easier to care for than informal pools since they rarely have an abundance of border decorations in the form of rocks, shrubs, bushes, and gangplanks. The typical formal pool is usually decorated with **water lilies** , most of which successfully winter and reappear the following spring. They can be enhanced with **tropical water lilies** which only live for the summer months in most areas, and die when the water gets too cold. Different tropical lilies have different temperature requirements. Water lilies are usually planted in tubs which can be removed in the fall or left over the winter.

Hardy lilies are very prolific and their potato-like tuberous roots can be broken apart and new plants easily started. That's about all there is to the formal pool except for adding water during periods when the rainwater doesn't equal the evaporation rate. In most cases, a garden hose will suffice, rather than building in an automatic water leveler like you probably have in your bathroom toilet.

So, while formal pools are easier to maintain, they are more expensive than informal ponds. Yet, they allow for enhancing the architecture of your home...and they look expensive.

Miniature pools

Old bathtubs, refrigerator liners, barrels or wine casks all make a container which is effective as a miniature pool. The container is merely buried in the ground and you have a ready-made garden pond.

It's not quite easy, though. Most of the containers mentioned may still contain substances which are poisonous to fishes and plants. An old **bathtub** may have soap clinging invisibly to its surface; **barrels** may once have contained gasoline or oil. No, don't take a chance. Clean your containers thoroughly and then paint them. Here's how to do it.

First, scrub the container as clean as possible with a new, stiff scrubbing brush and white vinegar. Then fill it with water and allow the water to over-flow for as long as convenient, using a slowly running garden hose.

Informal ponds cost less and require little or no maintenance time although formal, well laid out ponds enhance the garden to a greater extent.

After an hour of this, add a lot of lime (the kind used for building purposes is fine). Let the lime sit for a day or so, then empty the container, rinse it once more in running water, and let it dry.

While it's drying, order some **rubber-base blue paint** from your pet shop or from the source of your water lilies and goldfish. Then paint the container with two heavy coats of the blue paint, allowing a few days in between for the paint to dry.

Now dig the hole and "plant the container" so it projects a few inches above the surface of the ground to prevent run-off from flooding it and washing in dangerous pesticides or fertilizers and washing out the fish! After a few days add a few small, inexpensive fish. If they live, your miniature pond is probably safe for the water lilies and the fishes. These small miniatures are a lot of

Healthy pond goldfish will breed in the right conditions and soon the owner will have more stock in the pond without extra cost!

A male will chase the female around for quite some time before the actual spawning takes place. Photos by J. Elias.

fun. In each family there might be children who would like to have their own little water garden. Or you might want to raise different kinds of fishes and keep them separated so they don't interbreed. In any case, it's a good way to get some experience in water gardening...and cheap enough!

The author's first garden ponds were old bathtubs. These were purchased from the local housewreckers and were very inexpensive. A series of four or five of them in a row, separated by irises, and decorated with a different color water lily in each, makes an attractive display.

The informal pond

The Informal pool or pond has a non-geometric border. Its irregular outline is part of its charm and it should be made to look as natural as possible. It is truly to be considered a "fake" pond and the idea is to make it as counterfeit as possible. The more it looks like it was created by nature, the more successful you were as its designer.

The usual informal pond is located at the lowest point in the terrain. This is usually where water accumulates anyway. Thus you have the advantage of having fishes in a pond where mosquitos might breed; the fishes eat the mosquito larvae before they hatch out and fly into your bedroom.

Informal ponds are always decorated with huge stands of shrubs, plants, rocks, gangplanks, ducks, swans, geese, lotus and walkways and paths surrounding them. There are, of course, many small informal ponds which usually have been adapted from pre-molded polyethylene or fiberglass containers. The author uses old refrigerator liners which he buries in the ground to grow live foods to feed his aquarium fishes. These could also be used for garden pools, too.

The use of **children's wading pools** is not recommended because they break down and leak. Usually they are made of material that cannot tolerate cold or freezing, and they crack in the winter. If stones are thrown at the fish (kids!!!!), the stones might perforate the liner and allow it to leak. Stay with the molded or formed product. ASK YOUR PETSHOP TO GET ONE FOR YOU.

Some plastics are poisonous and not suitable for an aquarium environment. **Tropical Fish Hobbyist magazines** usually contain advertisements for fiberglass or molded plastic pools.

In general, keep your pond away from trees for the tree often contains birds and their droppings are usually not pleasant. Then, too, fish-eating birds can pounce from a near branch into your pond and fly off with one of your prized specimens. But the main problem with trees is that they shed their leaves into the pond, especially in the fall, and certain leaves make the water very acid and dark (oak leaves especially).

When my lawn is mowed, the wind usually carries a lot of the grass clippings into the pool. I have encouraged this for more than 20 years and found that the small amount of occasional grass every week or so has proven to be very beneficial to the goldfish and koi.

The temporary pond

While it is hardly to be recommended, there are people who use swimming pools as goldfish or koi ponds. In almost every case, the owner of the artificial pool stops the filtering process when he stops using the pool. The water turns green and becomes laden with **mosquito larvae.** If he lets out the water, the pool collapses or might even be forced out of the ground by the presence of ground water, so he leaves in the water and throws in some fish to eat the algae and mosquito larvae. This usually works to a point. The goldfish or koi thrive in the environment as long as all the chemicals have disappeared from the pool, especially the copper sulfate which controls the algae and the chlorine. But if the fishes live for a week, then probably they are safe.

Sooner or later, though, the thought of a green-pea soup aquarium in your swimming pool will offend your senses enough to have you buy a cover for the swimming pool and keep it out of sight.

The author has seen, however, some clever conversions of swimming pools into magnificent formal ponds. But it is expensive and a major effort. An architect and engineer must be consulted and don't expect the pool filter to last long unless the plants are protected in burlap wrappings, for the filter will surely remove the soil in which they are planted.

The formal Oriental goldfish pond

In Hawaii and Japan there is much more call for a filtered, running water **koi** or **goldfish** pond than a swimming pool. Restaurants, hotels and larger homes are usually decorated with a pond of one sort or another. Many are quite elaborate and it is not unknown that the fishes in the pond are worth more than the home itself.

Oriental water gardens are magnificent as can be seen from the accompanying photographs, but don't be fooled. In all cases they are managed with a full time person dedicated to the care and cleanliness of the pond and its inhabitants. The basis of the pond is to observe the beauty of the fishes from being above them, thus goldfish and koi are evaluated for their finnage and colors AS SEEN FROM ABOVE. English-speaking peoples usually think of a pond as an extension of their aquarium and the side view of their fishes is very important to them even though they don't get to see these qualities while the fishes are in the pool.

In most cases, Oriental ponds have running water and this is the way the water is kept clean enough for the fishes to be visible. Roof drains are usually emptied into the fish pond and the overflow from the pond may be used for further garden irrigation or be emptied directly into the sewerage system. When enough rain water is

Oriental gardens are magnificent but they require much more mainte-nance than informal or simple formal ponds. Photo courtesy of Kodan-sha Ltd.

not available, other water sources are connected so the water remains clear and flowing. These Oriental ponds are usually over-stocked with fishes and the almost constant water changes serve more than cosmetic purposes: it serves to bring oxygenated waters to the fishes, too.

Running water is not good for water lilies. Thus Japanese and Hawaiian ponds almost never have such plants. Water lilies do best in standing water which gets as much sun as possible (never less than 4 hours). The more sun, the more flowers. In any case, this book is not the kind of book that will send you on your way to a successful Oriental pond. You really have to be fanatic about the fishes to enjoy an Oriental pond. Some Japanese koi and Chinese goldfish are worth a year's salary of an ordinary man...and some champion fish are worth a lifetime of a person's earnings.

This pool is suitable for home enthusiasts who simply wish to enjoy the pleasure of water and fish in the garden.

The waterfall effect achieved through use of the pipe creates a feeling of coolness on even the hottest day.

This book is for the everyday person who might wince at spending even a day's pay for a fish! Equal attention is paid to the fish and plants. Thus a "**garden pool**" is just that...a garden for the plants and a pool for the fish.

Emptying the pond

It's been known for a long time that, sooner or later, everything on earth that goes up, must come down. The same is true of a water garden. While, theoretically, there is never a need to change the water in a pond, there are certain practical circumstances which are best handled by **draining the pool.**

Those circumstances include, but are not limited to, flooding, poisoning, unsightly algae blooms, smelly decaying vegetation and dead fish as a result of the decaying vegetation, treatment of the pond for leaking or the removal of all the fishes because the quality of the strain is breaking down.

The easiest way to drain a pond is to use a pre-constructed drain made just for this purpose. This is, however, costly, rarely used, and hind-sight. Even though the author has built in drains (which always clog in the middle of the process), he relies upon rented pumps. Rental companies that specialize in building and home articles always have solutions for flooded basements and the like and they rent pumps for very reasonable prices if you want it for less than a day. Be sure that the pump has a filter or some device which will keep it from becoming clogged with the usual debris found in the bottom of a pond. Then, too, the rate of flow should not be too great since it might suck in fishes and roots of the plants. A typical sump pump works well.

If you actually empty a pond completely, use the occasion to repaint it, to cut up the lily tubers and reset them, to examine the goldfish and koi for parasites, and to examine the pond for any obvious repairs or replacements.

Building the pond

The scope of this book is rather limited and does not cover the details of constructing concrete or cement block ponds. The best book for that purpose is *GOLD-FISH POOLS, WATER LILIES, AND TROPICAL FISHES by Dr. G. L. Thomas, Jr.* It is available, or can be ordered, from the same shop in which you got this book.

In most cases the construction of a permanent formal pool involves the use of reinforced concrete or cement (cinder) blocks. These must be set onto a proper footing, about three feet into the ground. The digging, cement work and steel reinforcement are usually within the abilities of most local artisans and many people who are handy...and can follow the instructions to be found in great detail in *Dr. Thomas' GOLDFISH POOLS* book cited above, should not have any trouble with the construction. There is, however, one word of caution: BUILD THE BEST, STRONGEST POND YOU CAN AFFORD. The catastrophe of a badly leaking pond because the bottom or sides cracked can hardly be compensated with the meager savings you enjoyed at the beginning. A leaking pool constantly drains and must be constantly refilled...and it constantly aggravates. Do yourself a favor. Build it right, even if it has to be smaller than you first planned.

Accessories

There are certain accessories which you may want to consider. **Underwater lights** which are usually made for swimming pools, can be fitted into the formal or informal pool simply by attaching them to a cement block and letting them lay on the bottom with the light directed wherever you desire. This light also serves as a warning light to children and animals.

A **submersible pump** can be installed in a sump (a hole deeper than the pond itself) to drain the pool or some of its contents when it gets cloudy or foul.

A **spray** which shoots water into the air is also available. It does aerate the water but usually it disturbs the growth of the water lilies and it agitates the surface of the water so the fishes are hardly visible.

Taro are ideal tub plants to situate around the garden pool. Photo by Charles Masters.

Subgravel filter, heaters and **flowerpots** are other things to consider. None of these accessories are necessary...none are important...all have their drawbacks and the author doesn't recommend any of them.

What the author does recommend are beautiful water and bog plants...and magnificent goldfish and koi.

3.
Plants

The first things that a garden pond brings to mind are **water lilies.** There are basically two types of water lilies and each type has many varieties. The very interesting fact is that these two types of lilies, the **hardy** and **tropical,** look alike, act alike, grow alike...and yet they have never been crossed, one to the other.

Plants and fish can be combined in certain ponds to good effect and help to make the display become an integral part of the garden. Photo by Dr. H. R. Axelrod

Hardy water lilies are perennials. Plant them correctly the first time and they will return every spring with more vigor and more flowers. The author makes a little profit on his lilies. Every spring he removes the mesh plastic basket containing the tubers. The baskets are taken apart, the roots cut away and the tubers cut into pieces. Then the tubers are replanted in humus, earth and nutrient, put into a very loosely woven potato or onion sack, weighted down with a few bricks and put back into the basket. Then they are replanted usually in March. By May the flowers have appeared once again...and the tubers which were in excess are sold through the local petshop for a handsome profit.

Hardy lilies live nicely through the winter provided they are planted deeply enough so the tuber doesn't freeze. After two or three years, however, they begin to lose the depth of their color and should be replaced. When the tubers are removed and repotted, they do much better. The author has had the same lilies for more than 25 years; they are still very colorful, but every second year they have their roots trimmed and the tubers are thinned out.

Hardy lilies are available either through petshops who order exactly what you wish, or by mail order. It's much better to buy from your local petshop for then they are obligated to supply you with advice and a guarantee of sorts. **Guarantees** with anything living are quite difficult, but you'll need a source of goldfish, koi, water plants, fish food, etc., so you might just as well start out at your neighborhood aquarium petshop and make their acquaintance.

Hardy lilies are usually available in sizes from about 3″ in diameter to some which reach 12″ in diameter. These diameters refer, of course, to their flowers and leaves...generally speaking, the smaller the leaf, the smaller is the flower. Hardies are found in almost every shade of color except blue and black. Many hardies have floating flowers; some have flowers which reach above the surface of the water. Almost all hardies have smooth-edged leaves and many have a lovely fragrance. They are excellent as cut flowers, but very short lived.

As a rule, hardies open their flowers about 11 a.m. and close their flowers about 6 hours later. They begin flowering in May in New Jersey where the author resides.

Tropical water lilies are annuals. They usually are grown the same as the hardies, but the tropical usually grows faster and requires a lot more space than a hardy. Their leaves and flowers are usually much larger than the hardies, too, and their leaves are not usually smooth edged but scalloped. Tropicals occur in many different colors...even blues and purples which almost reach black but not quite. Yellow is, however, a very rare color for all water lilies.

Tropicals have one peculiar characteristic. They must be planted when the pond water is warm, say at least 60°F. This is about June in New Jersey. Then in late July they begin to bloom with magnificent glory. The author mixes them with hardies. By late September when the hardies begin to fade, the tropicals are still blooming...and when the hardies are all gone by October 15th, the tropicals still throw off an occasional flower. This is when they are to be removed, trimmed and stored in a cool, dark (preferably damp) place until they are planted the following June...or January if you live in the southern hemisphere.

Generally speaking, tropicals are much stouter than hardies and their flowers are usually raised above water level except for the small lilies from Sri Lanka which are sometimes offered as aquarium specimens.

Tropical water lilies occur in two varieties...the day blooming lilies and the night blooming lilies. **Day bloomers** have their flowers open about the same as hardy lilies, say from 11 a.m. to 5 p.m. The **night bloomers** open about an hour after the day bloomers close, say 6-7 p.m. and stay open all night until about the time the day bloomers open, say 11 a.m. So, by mixing your lilies properly, you can always have something beautiful to look at...day or night!

The only disadvantage of night bloomers is they rarely, if ever, have any fragrance, at least most of the common ones do not have fragrance, so, should fragrance be important to you be sure to inquire about this attribute prior to buying it.

Tropical lilies, even though they are more temperature sensitive than hardies, are larger, stronger, and grow better. They easily and readily hybridize with other tropicals; that's why we have so many different colors. But tropicals do have their minimum requirements as regards temperature and size of available growing space. Because they are temperature sensitive, they must first be planted in fairly shallow water...and as they get larger they should be moved to deeper and deeper water. This is a nuisance for many water gardeners who live in temperate or colder than temperate zones, but for the water gardners who live in the tropics, tropical water lilies act the same as hardies. They bloom continuously all year and reach fairly large size.

Lilies in flower are beautiful and the floating leaves provide the fish with valuable shade from direct sunlight, so the plant has twofold benefits. Photo courtesy of Van Ness Water Gardens.

Cultivated Iris are outstanding marginal or bog plants and can be grown very easily at the water's edge. Photo courtesy of Van Ness Water Gardens.

Some tropical water lilies are **viviparous**, that is, they bear living young. The young plants grow from the center of certain "mother" leaves. This is a very rare characteristic among plants...even among fishes, but live-bearing fishes are real aquarium favorites.

There are about 100 different kinds of day-blooming and 50 kinds of night-blooming tropical water lilies, with new varieties appearing on the market every year...like roses.

Other aquatic and bog plants

Your local aquarium store has plenty of **aquatic plants.** Mostly, they are used in aquariums and are submerged and tropical. Thus they will perish every fall and require replanting in the spring. There are also many hardy aquatic and bog plants which can hibernate over the winter and show up again in the spring.

Arrowhead, Papyrus, Iris, Cat-tail, Umbrella-palm and Green Taro are just a few of the **bog plants** which will grow out of the water and might well winter and show growth the following year. Even the submerged forms like *Anacharis, Cabomba, Myriophyllum, Ludwigia, Vallisneria, Sagittaria,* etc., will usually last through the winter but many water gardeners consider these as pests rather than as decorations. It's a matter of taste...and your local petshop will probably welcome your bringing these plants in for him to sell. The pet shop refers to the submerged plants as **"bunch" plants** because they are usually planted in bunches in the aquarium.

Ask your petshop to get you specialized plants for the bog. Tell him that you'd really rather have plants which die over the winter so that you can change the decor.

Once a plant "takes," such as papyrus, it's very difficult to get rid of since it is very adventitious and its roots travel all around the pond.

How to plant

The way to plant your garden pool depends upon the kind of pool and when you intend to plant it. For a new, formal pool, you might care to plant right on the floor of the pool. This is not especially recommended, but it can be done. Once the pool has been planted, add 6″ of good soil and then cover that with three inches of coarse gravel or sand...the kind that your petshop sells for the aquarium. Plant the **water lily tubers** and slowly add WARM (75-80°) water until the tops of the lily tubers are covered. Sometimes (mostly) the tubers have already started to sprout, so handle them carefully. If you use cold water, the tubers might go into shock and while this may not kill them (it rarely does) it may stunt their growth for several months.

As the tuber grows shoots, add more and more water until the pool is full. The idea is to let the sun's rays hit the growing plant and keep it warm. The bottom of the pool will eventually become one tangled mass of roots and if you ever want to get rid of a particular plant it will be very difficult. That's why **movable containers** are suggested.

If you plant your lilies or other plants in movable containers there are many advantages. The most important advantage is that you can plant the tubers and other plants in a comfortable position. Once the container is set, you merely lower it into the water. Every fall, when the plant hibernates, you can remove the containers, take out the tubers, trim them, sell some or repot them.

You can also readily rid yourself of any plant that doesn't suit your fancy.

There is another very good reason for using containers. Very often you may have to get into the pool and wade. Perhaps someone has dropped a ring into the pool...or, more likely, you want to **catch some of the fish** and sell them. To do this you want to use a seine or net. If you walked on the muddy bottom in which you planted the tubers you would not only make a horrible mess but you might well kill the plant by squashing the roots. Having been planted in a container, the roots are well protected.

It is a good idea to put the **container** on a cinder (cement) block to keep it off the bottom. This allows a good hiding place for the fish that need it (like babies) and the breeders often spray their eggs on it.

For those with a **natural pond on a farm,** you are still advised to use movable containers. Not only can you remove the plants and shift them around, but horses or cattle will walk around a container whereas they will trample anything planted in the mud. Still another reason for using a **movable container** is that they are easier to fertilize. You can lift them out of the water in the fall and add humus or liquid fertilizer to the pot and keep it in your basement where it is cold and dark while the plant hibernates over the winter in damp soil. Keep it from drying out! Don't let it freeze either.

Your water garden supplier or petshop will be able to get you special cedar planting tubs and pails but most people use plastic laundry baskets which have lots of holes in them. Even plastic milk delivery containers are useful if you can get them easily. Be careful, though, as some plastics are toxic and some woods are harmful. Redwood, for example, discolors the water and inhibits the growth of most water lilies.

The potting medium

What you plant your lily tubers in is very important. For many reasons use a regular **potting loam** or **garden soil**. Be sure there is no clay, peat moss or decaying wood in it. If you cannot find any potting soil, then dig your own from your garden. Try to find some commercial dried **cow manure** as it is the best fertilizer for both the water lilies and the garden pond itself since it promotes the growth of infusoria which feeds the water "fleas" (*Daphnia*) which feeds the goldfish, especially the small ones. Use the cow manure in a 10% mixture by weight (10 pounds of soil plus one pound of manure).

There are many other **fertilizers** but the problem with them is that they dissolve in the water and are thus not readily available for the plant roots. Stick with the commercial cow manure; if you live near a farm don't be tempted to use fresh manure of any type. It will be too rich and over-fertilize your pond water and make it a stinking, slimy mess. (But it will grow great *Daphnia* and other small water "bugs".)

The advice given above is far from the last word on potting media...but if you stick with this advice you won't go wrong. Experimentation just isn't worth the price of a fouled up garden pool.

The tubers

Lilies grow from "bulbs" or **tubers**; some people call them **rhizomes**. In any case they grow from a thick

If the aquatic plants are potted in the correct medium they will thrive and enhance the pool. Photo by M. Gilroy.

Waterfalls, whilst disturbing aquatic plants, are beneficial to the fishes because of the increased oxygen created by the action. Photo by M. Gilroy.

fleshy rootstock and the rootstocks usually appear as a tiny bulb (*stellata* from Sri Lanka, for example), as a long, skinny potato-like root (*ordorata*, for example), or spiny long, thin sweet potato-like roots (such as *tuberosa*, for example), or a mass of thick roots like Marliac hybrids which are basically crosses between *odorata* and *tuberosa*. Each of these (except for *stellata*) has "eyes" in the rhizome like potatoes. These eyes sprout, each eye capable of producing a new plant.

When you get your first tubers from your local petshop, or from wherever they are grown, they will either be *starters*...that is rhizomes without any sign of life, or *sprouters* which have growing stems and leaves and, perhaps, a few buds.

The first thing to do is to examine them carefully. Squeeze them...they should be as hard as a new potato, perhaps a bit spongier. But you should not be able to squash them. Smell them. They should have a fresh scent, like soil, and not of rotting vegetation. Plant them as soon as possible and in no case allow them to lay out in the sun to dry out. If you cannot plant them immediately, wrap them in soaking wet newspaper, burlap or even an old towel. Keep them moist!

Now, assuming your soil is already in your planting containers, you are ready to **plant the tubers.** Scoop out a hole about 1½"deep and lay the tuber in a natural position. The growing point should extend up. Very carefully, cover the tuber with the soil you removed. The tuber should now be about 1" deep with the growing point protruding. Now cover the pot again using very large gravel, say about the size of a pea. This is to keep the goldfish from digging into the pot and disturbing the soil. It also helps in keeping the tuber from floating away. At this stage you can wet the whole thing down and pack it tightly by pressing all around the **growing points.** DO NOT BREAK THE GROWING POINTS!

Since, in most cases, the tuber will float loose unless you used enough sand or gravel, you are advised to use a stone or brick to lay over the tuber (but not over the growing point) to hold it down. The author has a technique which has never failed him. Using a piece of burlap with very wide mesh, put a brick on the bottom of the burlap which now lines the planting container. The soil and tuber are placed in position and then, not using sand, the ends of the burlap are gathered and loosely tied together around the growing point which extends out of this purse. Thus nothing floats up and the goldfish cannot disturb it. This burlap purse technique is also ideal for planting in natural ponds, too.

The **depth** in which you plant can be important. If there are already stems, buds and leaves, plant them so the leaves float. Keep lowering the container as the stems get longer. Don't be too concerned about the depth as a few inches is not very important. The leaves grow very fast and if they are set a few inches too deep, their rapid growth will soon have them above the water level and floating.

Like everything that is potted, you must be sure that you have enough **growing space** for the lilies you have selected. How much space? Not too much and not too little. The test is as follows:

Find out how large the leaf will grow and use a container that is at least 4 leaves square and 3 leaves deep. The more space you give the plant, the better it will grow. There is no such thing as too much space for the roots...there's only too little.

The suggestions made here are the ideal. Lilies are rather hardy. You can plant them too deep in pots that are too small, and without proper fertilizer, and they'll still grow and be very beautiful, but at least make an effort to allow the tropical lilies twice as much room as the hardies...they need it.

Plant propagation

Don't get involved in fancy water lily planting in a small garden pool. It won't work. It takes lots of experiments to get what you want and hardly anyone with a small set-up is successful. In any case, don't try to cross a hardy with a tropical. It has never worked. Also, day-bloomers don't cross with night-bloomers either!

The best way to **propagate water lilies** is with vegetative propagation. This means that you retrieve the rootstocks and cut them into pieces. It's almost just that easy.

Here's how it works: unless you have removed the tubers in the late fall, the best time is the spring. Hardies can actually be removed any time and divided, but the spring is the best time because psychologically you will probably be more industrious and interested in getting things going.

Every three or four years, whether you like it or not, **you must divide the rootstocks.** If you don't they will gradually fade and produce smaller and smaller flowers. By constantly dividing them, replanting and refertilizing them, you will get their maximum production. Here's how it's done: Remove the **movable container** and empty its contents in as unobtrusive a place as possible. The garden patch is probably the best place. Using a garden hose, try to wash away all the soil and expose the rootstock. Clean it as much as you can. You must be able to recognize the "eyes" like the eyes on a sprouted potato (which is also a tuber). Now **cut** the rhizomes, tubers, rootstocks, or whatever you may care to call them, into 5″ chunks. Make sure each chunk has at least one eye which is sprouting. To cut them use a very sharp, heavy serrated knife or a hacksaw. Don't chop them.

Now you can plant them and start all over again with very active healthy plants with lots of growth potential. If you have a good rapport with your local petshop owner, he'll probably be interested in buying your excess rootstocks from you. Wrap them carefully in wet newspaper and label them with the type of lily that they are...especially the color and whether it is a day- or night-bloomer.

As a youngster (in Bayonne, N.J.), the author would plant every pond he could find with water lilies. He used milk containers, the kind that held a dozen quarts of milk. Then every spring he would harvest the rhizomes and sell them to a local (Staten Island) goldfish supplier who sold them as "home grown" lilies. By the time the author was 17 (in 1944), he had enough money to buy a car! Isn't that the dream of every 17 year old?

4.
Fishes

There are two basic kinds of fishes which are kept in garden pools...**koi** and **goldfish**. Huge books have been written about each of these kinds of fishes and you are invited to look at these books at your local petshop.

Goldfish give the water a real splash of color and are available in many strains and color forms. They are easy to maintain and do not require exact conditions.

Right now we'll just cover the main points.

Goldfish and **koi** (Japanese colored carp) were developed in China and Japan. They were prized for their color and finnage **when viewed from above**. This was were around 500 years before man even dreamt of an aquarium. Some of them are extremely valuable. The more expensive they are, the more delicate they are. This is especially true of the goldfish.

There are many **other kinds of fishes** that you can keep in your garden pond, but none of them are as colorful or as hardy as koi and goldfish. If you live in the tropics where the water temperature won't drop below 70°F., then you'll be able to keep just about any fish which you buy at your local aquarium shop. If you live in more temperate zones, then you can probably keep anything caught in the nearest stream. (Check with the local authorities before you go fishing for them.)

Whether you like it or not, sooner or later your garden pool will probably be host to **snails, snakes** and **frogs.** None of these are dangerous except for snakes and they are more afraid of you than you are of them...just ignore them. They'll eat their fill of fish and go away by themselves when it gets too cold. If you have children, call the local authorities who deal with wild animals and ask them to remove the snake from your pool. The author usually catches them by baiting a small goldfish with a fine iron hook through its back. The goldfish is attached to a long thin piece of nylon fishing line. The snake usually gets the bait at night and swallows it. The snake is then pulled from the pond, dangling and squirming, and disposed of in the nearest body of water. The hook will eventually dissolve or rust away and the snake will live happily ever after.

Koi are the jewels of the garden pool but they are more expensive than gold-fish and require a good water quality only large filters can provide. Photo courtesy of Kodansha Ltd.

Goldfish

For the casual garden pool owner, the choice of occupants for your pond can usually be found at your **local aquarium store,** especially in the spring. Be careful when you select the goldfish for your pool...make sure you are not buying goldfish which originated in Singapore or some other tropical place, as many, many fancy varieties of goldfish have been produced in Singapore, Indonesia and other warm-water areas. These goldfish usually die when the water gets cold. On the other hand, if you are a real goldfish lover, you can remove the fish in the fall and let them winter in your aquarium.

There are several kinds of goldfish: goldfish with fancy fins; goldfish with fancy colors; goldfish with fancy eyes; and, finally, goldfish with fancy body shapes.

Goldfish often show patterns in which a number of different colors are combined on one fish.

Goldfish varieties or developed strains are attractive although "beauty is in the eye of the beholder." Short-bodied or fantail goldfish are not as hardy as comet goldfish for the garden pool. Photo K. Paysan.

There are also normal goldfish. No one really knows where goldfish come from. Almost every country has a residual population of goldfish which originated when some fish lover thought it would be less cruel to dump them in the local pond than to feed them to the family cat. These goldfish always return to the normal, wild type without fancy eyes, fins or colors. They are, simply, the **common goldfish** which almost are universal in their appeal. For your garden pool you should stick to the more common varieties of goldfish.

The common goldfish looks like an ordinary fish except that it has a basic golden reddish color. Some have black and some are albino. Stick with the most common...which are also the cheapest.

There are some "fancy" varieties which do well in garden pools. The **Comet** goldfish is one with a larger, longer body and a longer tail than the **common**. This enables it to jump and many a Comet has jumped out of the pool and dried out on the ground. Keep this in mind.

Another fancy is the **Fantail goldfish**. This was developed in Japan. It usually has two tails and two anal fins. Poor quality fantails have tails and anal fins which are joined at the base...it really doesn't matter for the average water gardener. The swimming movement of the **Japanese fantail** is slow and deliberate like a Japanese maiden in tight shoes and a tight kimono.

The **Japanese fantail** was further developed so the fins got longer and the body got chunkier. This fish was called a **Veiltail**. It takes several years for these magnificent fish to reach their full glory! But they are beautiful. It is also very slow moving and easily caught by fish-eating birds and snakes. You can also probably catch them with your bare hands; they may be hardy enough to survive a winter outdoors. Try it.

The **Shubunkin** is a Japanese goldfish having originated from the basic common goldfish stock. It is characterized by being multicolored and while they rarely are identically colored, they are readily recognized by their multicolored pattern. They are attractive, lively and hardy. They are to be recommended for the garden pool and are colorful enough for the aquarium as well.

Similar in coloration to the **Shubunkin** is the **Calico**. This fish was developed by the Chinese and appears in various body forms. Perhaps the most beautiful of all goldfish varieties is the **Calico Telescope-eyes**. This is a colorful fish with long fins like a normal fantail, but the eyes are not protruding. Of course there are **normal**

50

Telescope-eyed goldfish colored like a normal fish.

An all black goldfish has been developed. It is called a **Moor**. It is very hardy thus they are relatively inexpensive. They should be added to your collection. They readily breed with normal goldfish and often many of the offspring are black. Another weird goldfish is the **Celestial**. This fish is similar to the **Telescope** but their eyes not only protrude but are turned upward, always looking towards the heaven, thus their name. Another very uncommon goldfish is the **Water Bubble-eye**. This is a fish with bags hanging under each eye. It is not recommended for the garden pool since it is so delicate, but garden pool experts do attempt to keep them under special conditions of a shallow pool with a soft (plastic) bottom and sides. Sharp objects injure the bubbles and the fish suffers fatal eye infections.

Then there are the goldfish with growths on their heads. The most popular of these types of goldfish is the **Lionhead**. It has a growth over the head and around the eyes. It does not have a dorsal fin. The **Oranda** is a **Lionhead** with a dorsal fin. This is a very beautiful variety and experts are very successful with this fish in a garden pool. They have beautiful fins and swim well, quite in contrast to the **Lionhead**. Special varieties of **Oranda** have been developed with stark white bodies and red caps on their heads. They have many names, like **Redcaps, Strawberry heads** and the like. Some do well in garden pools but they are much more expensive than the common goldfish.

To summarize: If you are a beginner, stick with the more common varieties such as the Common goldfish , Shubunkins, Comets, Moors and Fantails. If you really want the fancy varieties keep them in an aquarium.

Koi, Japanese Colored Carp

Carps have been bred for many years and form an important part of the diet of eastern European cultures. They are bred by the millions and, due to their hardiness, are often sold alive in fish stores in Israel, Poland, Germany and neighboring countries. The Japanese also bred them for food but in the process they developed them in many color varieties. Over the years the cult of koi breeding has become a fascination in Japan and koi shows are held throughout the Japanese empire.

Koi breeding is not difficult but they rarely breed true to form. Koi are very hardy and are highly recommended for the larger garden pool. Koi grow much larger than goldfish, often reaching five pounds in weight. Since very rare color combinations are eagerly sought, the culls have little value. In Japan, the culls are discarded. In most other countries they are sold when fairly small, about the size of an adult goldfish, and they are only slightly more costly than fully grown goldfish.

Koi come in almost every **color** of the rainbow including such unbelievable colors as metallic gold and metallic silver. They can live for very long periods and they freely breed in most garden pool situations. Of course most of the fry are eaten by the fish in the pool, but a few always manage to escape.

As **newborn fry** they are usually an unattractive gray-green, but they soon develop into their characteristic colors. Multi-colored koi are rarely patterned in a standard color except for the solid colored ones. Thus the number of colors and the pattern generate the name by which the Japanese identify them. The colored photographs show many of the varieties available, but the author has written a very large book about koi (**Koi of the World**) and if these fish intrigue you by all means scan through a copy at your local petshop or public library.

5.
Feeding

Goldfish and koi eat the same things. While they are scavengers in nature, always scrounging around the bottom, they can hardly thrive in your garden pool under such circumstances. Most petshops sell pool food. Not

You can really get to know your fish through a regular feeding pattern and once they are tame the goldfish and koi will eat right out of your hand.

all of this food is to be recommended. When you feed your pet fish in your garden pool you want to see them, thus the best type of pool food is the kind that is **pelletized** and **floats**.

Goldfish and koi can be trained to eat out of your hand. You do this by feeding them as early in the morning as possible; always in the same place. At first they will be wary of you. Simply stay quietly and allow a few pellets to fall from your hand onto the surface of the water. As the pellets float away, a few brave fish will dash to the surface and grab the morsel. Over the course of a few weeks they will come closer and closer until finally they will actually fight over taking them directly from your hand. Don't worry about being bitten...they have no teeth on their outer lips!

The author's fish are so tame that they actually **stick their heads out of the water** and take dry pellets from his hand! It's not trick. With patience you can do the same thing. Every spring, once the ice thaws and the fish start eating again, the training must begin all over again. Goldfish and koi are hardly intelligent animals.

One of the advantages of this kind of feeding is that you never **overfeed**. While overfeeding is not a problem for the fish, that is, no fish will ever eat more than it needs, the uneaten food might **foul the water**. Then, too, as the water gets colder in the winter, the fish stop eating and become very inactive. When they stop coming for food, stop feeding them. They can go all winter without food. There has never been a case of any fish dying in the winter from starvation if they are well fed during the rest of the year.

By patiently waiting for the fish to seek you out the rewards are marvelous; here the koi is taking food from its owner. Photo by Dr. Herbert R. Axelrod.

While pelletized food is good enough for keeping the goldfish and koi alive, they really should have some living foods in order to keep them supplied with the raw materials which enhance their colors. The best food for them is what the Japanese call "michinko." Most English-speaking people call them *Daphnia* or **water fleas** (they are not fleas at all). Your local aquarium shop will probably have them from time to time. Just throw them into your pond. What the fish don't eat immediately will be eaten later. The *Daphnia* will live very well in the pond.

Daphnia are usually to be found in most ponds which do not have fishes in them. If you become very enthusiastic about your pool you can catch your own *Daphnia* by buying a long-handled *Daphnia net* and scooping them out of the water. There are books available at your petshop which discuss *Daphnia* and the other small animals living in ponds and which are suitable for fish foods.

So popular are *Daphnia* that they are sold frozen and freeze-dried. The chitinous shells on these animals bring out the reds in goldfish and koi, so should you find your fish are getting dreary, try some live foods for them.

CAUTION: When introducing live foods, you might also be introducing parasites and other dangerous animals like leeches and aquatic beetles which prey upon small fishes.

This is a very low grade risk since goldfish and koi are very hardy. Should you see a fish in your pool with anything attached to its body, merely remove the fish and, while holding it in the net, simply use tweezers to remove the parasite. There are lots of books on diseases of fishes, but your consolation is that goldfish and koi rarely fall victim to such diseases if they are properly maintained.

6.
Maintenance

The best way to have a **healthy pool** is to start with one. Be sure that the water is clean and fresh. Preferably take it from your local water supply and fill the pool with a garden hose. Allow the water to set for a week

Bright, clean water is all the fish ask for once they are well fed and given room to swim around in. Regular, partial water changes via the hose pipe during the warm months will ensure that a moderate sized pool remains in good condition.

before you introduce either fish or plants. **Sterilize** the fishes and plants in a solution of water and potassium permanganate. Make a solution of 1/8 grain of potassium permanganate in one U.S. gallon of water. Let the fishes and plants soak in it for 1-2 hours. The water you use should be the same temperature as that in the pool. The temperature in the pool should be the same as the temperature in the plastic bag containing the goldfish. This is easy to do. Merely float the goldfish in the plastic bag in which you brought them from the petshop, on top of the pool. In an hour the temperature should be the same. If you use water lilies you won't have to **sterilize** the tubers as they almost never contain parasites.

Keep your pool fresh and clean. If it is small enough, run some fresh water into it every week. Allow the water to splash into the pool, thus aerating it. Don't worry too much if your water turns a bit green, that is only **algae**. As your lilies grow and spread their leaves over the surface, the light will be reduced thus starving the algae. In very rare cases the algae will be so thick that a green scum will form. This can be taken out with a net. At this stage the water should be changed more often as the pool is too rich in nutrients, probably because you overfed the fish and uneaten particles are decaying and thus feeding the algae with nutrients, or you used too much fertilizer when you planted the lilies. Keep your eyes on your fishes. When they come to be fed you should be sure they are active and colorful and that their fins are held upright. Drooping fins are a sure sign something is going wrong.

One of the miracles of a pool is that **water changes** almost always solve mysterious problems. If you have any doubt about the health of your pool, allow your garden hose to run for a week with a small trickle of water. Of course you have to take care of the run-off or overflow. If you didn't make a provision for this merely scoop out a few bucketfulls of water from the pond and let fresh tap water slowly fill it up again. Water changing usually kills algae and most other small organisms because of the minute amounts of chlorine and fluorine in usual tap water. DO NOT ADD CHLORINE...EVER...TO YOUR POND except for the minute amounts which are contained in drinking water.

If you begin finding **dead fish** floating in your pond you might have a **disease** or epidemic, but more usually it is a case of having too many fish or too little aeration of the pond. First be sure that the water doesn't have an obnoxious odor (if it does, change it as quickly as you can with a running garden hose). Then keep the water dripping into the pond while you contact your local aquarium shop. Perhaps they can come over and see what's wrong. It is usual to have a dead fish now and then, but when you see 2 or 3 fish in a week you should look for something serious.

Should you find **mass deaths**, there are usually common-sense explanations. Your neighbor has spread weed-killer and some was carried by the air onto your goldfish pool. Or, perhaps, somebody sprayed fertilizer from an airplane a mile away and the wind carried it into your pond. Or, more than likely, somebody threw a cigar or cigarette into the pool. This might kill all the fish if the pond is small. All of these conditions can be corrected with rapid water changing.

If, on the other hand, your fishes are covered with **parasites,** or have **bloody blotches** on their body, there is little you can do to the pool itself. Your best bet is to use a small wading pool made of plastic and fill it with warm tap water. Allow the water to cool to the same temperature as the pool and add the chemical treatments which your petshop owner prescribes. In the worst case, most of your fishes will perish in the pond itself. Remove the dead bodies and change the water. Wait a week and start all over again.

The only times the author has ever known this to happen is with poisoning from sources mentioned above, or from a pool which was painted with a lead base paint instead of a rubber base paint, or that copper plumbing was used to bring water into the pond and the copper salts from the pipes poisoned the pool. If this is the case, then the plants will die too.

Ending the book with such **discouraging words** is not intended to warn you that these problems are common. It is extremely rare that any of these things will happen. Perhaps you will never have any bad experiences...but it's always good to know what to do in cases of emergencies.

ENEMIES

Sad to say, the fish (and to a lesser extent the plants, too) that live in garden pools have many enemies. Apart from the parasites and pathogenic organisms that can live in the water, a number of animals will actively prey on the fish. Exactly which animals will give you the most trouble of course depends on where you live—but just about every area has at least a few fish predators.

In Great Britain, for example, herons often are a problem, and in the United States raccoons and water snakes and frogs—not to mention herons and other birds as well—can be decidedly dangerous.

The following books are available from your petshop. Petshops carry a full range of pet books; they also have a lot of knowledge not to be found in books.

STARTING RIGHT WITH GOLDFISH
by Robert Gannon
ISBN 0-87666-081-2; **TFH M-504**
Full-color and black and white photos 5½ x 8½, *64 pages.*

GOLDFISH AND KOI IN YOUR HOME
Revised Edition
by Dr. Herbert Axelrod and William Vorderwinkler
ISBN 0-86622-041-0; **TFH H-909**
Contents: What Your Goldfish Need. Setting Up the Aquarium and Choosing the Plants. How to Choose Goldfish. Goldfish Varieties. How to Breed Goldfish. How to Raise Quality Goldfish. Goldfish Diseases. The Garden Pool. Koi, Japanese Imperial Colored Carp.
Audience: This comprehensive and very colorfully illustrated book discusses and shows many of the spectacular goldfish varieties existing today and provides readers with sensible ideas about how they can decorate their homes and gardens with tanks and pools of beautiful and hardy goldfish.
Contains more than 160 full-color photos, 20 black and white photos.
Hard cover; 224 pages, 5½ x 8½

GARDEN POOLS
by Paul Stetson
ISBN 0-87666-077-4; **M-513**
Full-color and black and white photos
5½ x 8½, *64 pages, soft cover*

GOLDFISH POOLS, WATER LILIES AND TROPICAL FISHES
by Dr. G. L. Thomas Jr.
ISBN 0-87666-080-4; **TFH H-919**
Contents: Planning For Your Pool. How to Construct a Concrete Pool. More Pool Designs. Curing the Pool. Water Lilies—Past and Present. The Hardy Water-Lilies. The Tropical Water-Lilies. Planting the Pool. Propagation. Culture and Winter Care. First Cousins of the Water-Lilies. Aquarium Water-Lilies and Other New Forms. Lists of "Bests." Accessory Aquatic Plants. Repairs, Maintenance, Pest and Disease Control. Building and Stocking the Farm Pond. All About Goldfish. Species and Varieties of Goldfish. Tropical Fish. Care and Feeding of Goldfish and Tropicals. All About Aquariums. Scavengers for Pools and Aquariums. Ailments and Enemies of Goldfish.
Audience: For anyone interested in keeping water lilies and other aquatic plants outdoors, with or without fish. Comprehensive and highly informative, but easy to read. Ages 15 and above.
Hard cover, 5½ x 8½ 336 pages
76 black and white photos, 90 color photos, 37 line illustrations